Recreational Ballroom, Cajun, and Country-Western Dance

Jerry Duke, Ph.D.

american press

BOSTON, MASSACHUSETTS

Copyright © 1996 by American Press
ISBN 0-89641-277-6

All rights reserved. No part of this publication may be reproduced, stored in a retrieval system, or transmitted, in any form or by any means, electronic, mechanical, photocopying, recording, or otherwise, without the prior written permission of the copyright owner.

Printed in the United States of America

Preface

Anthropologists and historians agree that dance has existed since the beginning of time. It is found among all human societies and serves a variety of purposes. People belonging to non-technical societies, for instance, dance for healing, worship, recreation, and communication. Animals and many insects have rituals that are also often described as dance. Plants go through rhythmic life processes which, if speeded up, would look like dance. Rhythmic movement is so basic and natural that it is one of the essentials of life.

The word "dance" conveys a different idea to each and every person. Even in the context of "ballroom dance," there are numerous ideas – from the graceful couples in their flowing dresses and handsome tuxedos dancing in a competition to couples merely socializing through dance.

Ballroom dance began in 16th century France and Italy. Ballroom dance is easy to recognize: two people dancing together, holding one another in a face to face position. When the music begins, these couples move about the dance area, keeping in step with the rhythm.

The basic ballroom dance position is well known. Partners face each other with one hand on each other's shoulder and the other hand joined to the side.

This book focuses on recreational ballroom dance. Students can learn ballroom dances in a very technical style for performance and competition or in a recreational style for social events. This book is written for students wanting to learn ballroom dances for recreation and will provide a good base for students who wish to later study for competion.

So find a partner, learn some moves, and get ready to have some fun!

J. Duke

Contents

1	**Introduction**	1
2	**Posture**	3
3	**Positions**	5
	Closed Position	5
	Semi-Open Position	7
	Reverse Semi-Open Position	8
	Open Position	10
	Reverse Open Position	11
	Swing Position	12
4	**Five Contact Points**	13
5	**Leading and Following**	15
	Guidelines	15
	Leading	16
	Following	18
6	**Rhythm**	19
	Music	19
	Dance	19
	Relating Dance to Music	20
7	**Teaching Sequence**	23
8	**Key to Abbreviations in Dance Descriptions**	27
9	**Cha-Cha**	29
	Basic Step	30
	Travel Step	30
	Crossover	31

	Half-Turn Chase	34
	Full-Turn Chase	36
	Arch Under	37
	Box Step	37
10	**Tango (American or Parisian)**	**39**
	Rhythm and Style	40
	Basic Step	40
	Corte	41
	Semi-Open	41
	Arch Under from Semi-Open	43
	Arch Under from Closed	43
	Open Reverse	43
	Closed Sweep	44
11	**Merengue**	**45**
	Basic Walk	45
	Sideways	45
	Arch Under	46
	Lock	46
	Pretzel	48
12	**Waltz**	**49**
	Rhythm	49
	Waltz Balance	50
	Traveling Waltz	50
	Box Step and Counter-Clockwise Turns	51
	Back-Step Turn	54
	Box Turn/Side-Turn Combination	55
	Traveling Cross-Step	55
13	**Swing**	**57**
	Rhythm and Style	58
	Position	59
	Basic Swing Step	60
	Arm Figures	60

	Arch Under and Return	60
	Double Arch Under	62
	Woman Turn Alone	62
	Woman Wrap	62
	Man Wrap	63
	Man Brush Off	64
	Step Sequence Variations	64
	Double Lindy	65
	BeBop	65
	Triple Lindy	65
	North Carolina Shag	66
14	**Foxtrot**	**67**
	Murray Magic Step	68
	Arch Under	68
	Semi-Open	69
	Clockwise Turn as Man Travels Forward	69
	Counter-Clockwise Turn as Man Travels Backward	70
	Zig-Zag	70
15	**Rumba**	**71**
	Rhythm and Style	71
	Closed Position	72
	Semi-Open Walk	73
	Arch Under	73
	Escort	73
16	**Samba**	**75**
	Basic Step Sequence	76
	Semi-Open	76
	Side Step	76
	Disco	76
17	**Mambo (Salsa)**	**77**
	Side Step	78
	Style Notes	78

18	**Cajun Dance**	**79**
	Cajun Two-Step	80
	Basic	80
	Basic with Travel	82
	Lake Charles (Louisiana) #1	82
	Lake Charles #2	83
	Lakes Charles #3	83
	Zydeco (Creole)	83
	Arm Figures	84
	Outside Arch Under	84
	Inside Arch Under	84
	Brush-Off	85
	Cajun Waltz	85
	Drive the Woman	85
	Cajun Cowb oy Waltz	86
	Six-Count Waltz	87
	Cajun Jitterbug	88
	Basic	89
	Travel	90
	Arm Figures	91
	Wrap and Exit	91
	Pretzel	91
	Zydeco Shuffle	93
19	**Country-Western Dance**	**95**
	Texas Two-Step	95
	Basic Sequence	96
	Couple 1/2 Turn Clockwise	97
	Couple Full Turn	98
	Arm Figures	98
	Cowboy Waltz	101
	Outside Arch Under	102
	Inside Arch Under	102
	Woman Walk Around	103

Chapter 1
Introduction

Couple dancing is believed to have evolved from line and circle dances in the 13th century in southern France. First, men and women danced holding opposite ends of a handkerchief; then, side by side with the woman's hand on the man's arm; and gradually more familiar positions appeared through the years until the early 1800s. Couples began to hold one another face to face and by the 1930s, marathon dancers actually took turns sleeping on each other's shoulders. Positions indicating even more familiarity have been observed, but are not yet widely accepted.

There was an extreme class structure during the Renaissance. Couple dancing was done by the peasants and as a performance art by the noble class. Even though the basic steps of the dances were similar, the style in which they were done was very different. The commoners would stamp, leap, and shout, while the nobles would bow and gracefully walk or hop to the music. Children of the nobility were given dancing lessons to become proficient at the social grace known as deportment. These ideas of posture and social graces are still a part of ballroom dance and an important aspects which make dance events a lot of fun.

Afro-Americans have had a great influence on ballroom dance as well as its music. They are largely responsible for many variations of the Swing dance and so-called "fad" dances. Recently there has been an intense interest in dances with a Latin American flavor. Dance teachers are always looking for something new and exciting and will sometimes invent a dance at a moment's notice hoping it will become popular.

This kind of dancing is an important form of communication between the sexes. Learning the basics and continuing to keep up with new trends will lead to a life of enjoyment. Students should keep in mind that the goal is to learn basic skills, but be willing to put every effort to learning and trying new movements. Ballroom dance takes practice just like any movement skill.

Chapter 2
Posture

Good posture and correct body alignment are important. Dancers look very good when they stand tall and appear in control. Movements are easier to execute and balance is easier to maintain when all the muscles used for alignment are active.

The head should be held high and straight so that an imaginary line or string from behind the ear would fall through the mid-shoulder and hip joints and, when standing still with the feet together, would continue down behind the knee cap to a point some two inches in front of the ankle bone. With this alignment as a base, hip and leg movements are easily controlled.

Main points to remember include:

1. Head is held high and straight over the body.
2. Shoulders are level.
3. Chest is lifted; abdomen is pulled inward.
4. Hips are aligned directly under the shoulders, but free to move when necessary.
5. Arms are held slightly away from the body and move with the shoulders.

6. Weight is over the balls of the feet whenever possible even though the heel may also be down.

THE "DRIP-LINE"

The body and legs should move at the same time. When a leg moves for a step, it should not move alone. The body should move in the same direction and at the same time. Think of being in the rain with an umbrella directly overhead and walk without letting the feet get out from under the umbrella. This imaginary circle of dry area on the floor under you can be thought of as the "drip-line." There are times that the reach of the foot is extended beyond this imaginary drip-line, but the dancer will move with much more balance and control and be able to lead and follow more easily if the "drip-line" concept is maintained.

Chapter 3
Positions

In addition to the positions described in this chapter, there are several other positions for social dance and many for couple folk dances. The positions in this chapter are the basic positions for use with social dance.

CLOSED POSITION

Partners stand facing each other slightly askew with shoulders and hips parallel. Each person should be able to look straight over his or her partner's right shoulder without turning the head. This will place the couple in a position so that each person's right foot is pointed toward the space between his or her partner's feet (Figure 3.1).

The man's left arm is extended comfortably to his left and slightly forward with the palm up so the woman can place her right hand, palm down, in his hand.

The man places his right hand under the woman's left arm and on her left shoulder blade. The woman's right arm is placed on top of the man's left arm (with very little pressure) and her hand on the man's left shoulder in such a way so she can push gently away for easy following. When first starting to practice, women should grasp the man's shoulder (gently) so that her thumb is in front (see Chapter 4 — Contact Points").

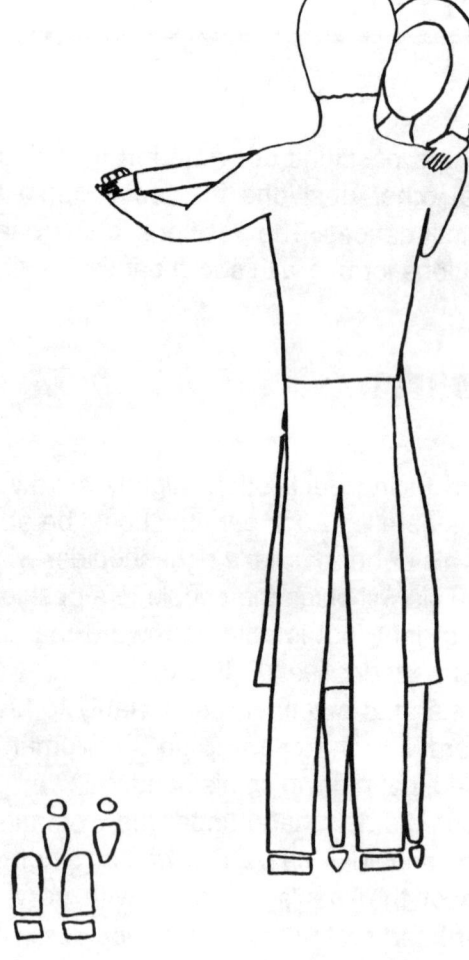

**Figure 3.1
Closed Position**

Positions

SEMI-OPEN POSITION

Holding the same as in closed position, both partners turn toward their outstretched arm (the woman turns right; the man turns left) so they are facing the same direction. The man's right and the woman's left elbows should bend to allow the shoulders to be closer (Figure 3.2).

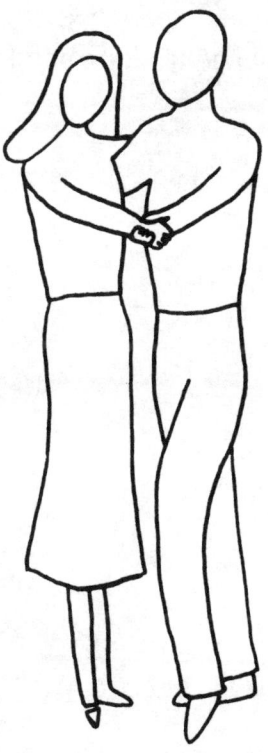

**Figure 3.2
Semi-Open Position**

REVERSE SEMI-OPEN POSITION (Tango)

From the semi-open or closed position, partners turn inward toward the reverse direction and adjust the arms. As a turn begins, the man circles his left arm counterclockwise upward and down from the elbow, allowing his hand to slide over the woman's right hand until both are pointed down. Meanwhile the man's right hand moves to the woman's upper arm (Figure 3.3). Some teachers prefer to have the man change his right hand to an outstretched hold.

**Figure 3.3
Reverse Semi-Open Position**

OPEN POSITION

Face the same direction as in semi-open position but turn loose of the leading hands and allow the free arms to hang by the sides (Figure 3.4).

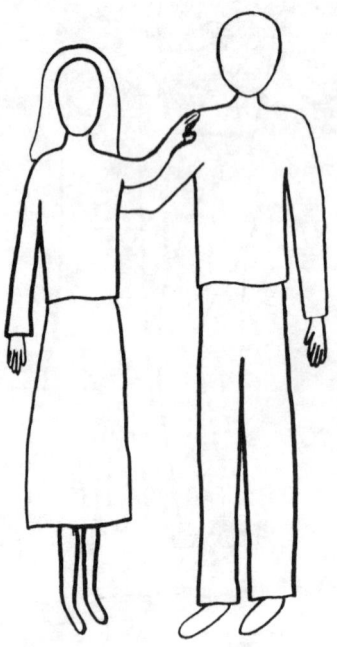

**Figure 3.4
Open Position**

REVERSE OPEN POSITION

Facing the opposite direction, the man's left hand holds the woman's right hand (Figure 3.5).

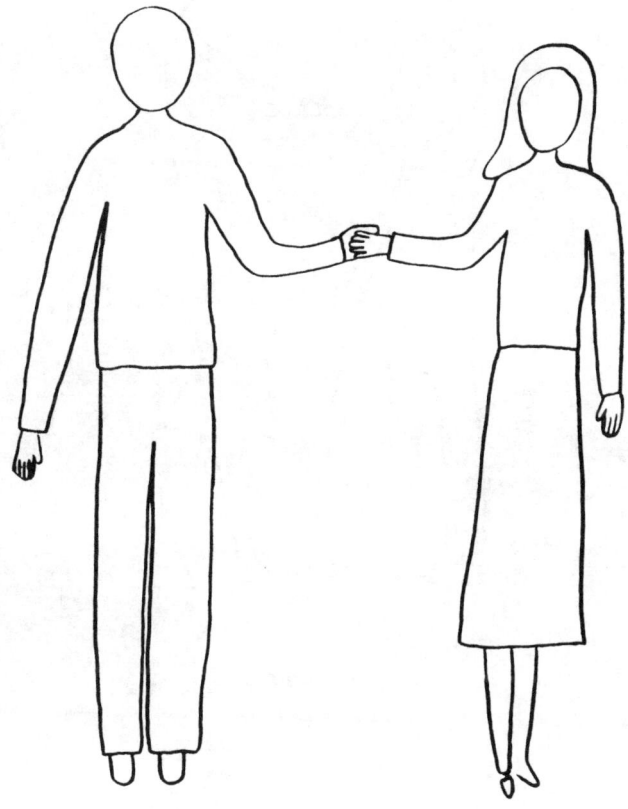

Figure 3.5
Reverse Open Position

SWING POSITION

Facing the partner, hold both hands (Figure 3.6).

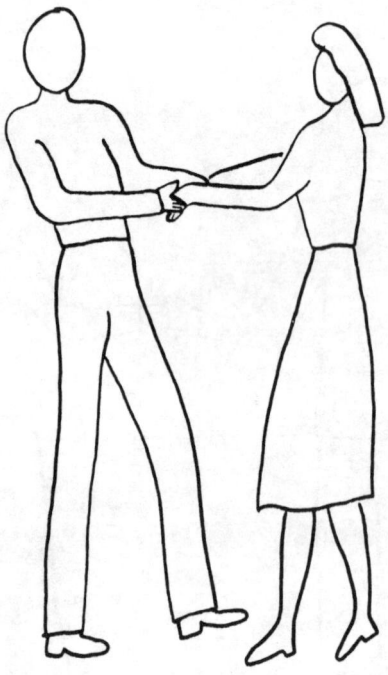

**Figure 3.6
Swing Position**

Chapter 4
Five Contact Points

In order of importance, the five contact points are:

1. The woman's left hand is on the man's right shoulder, held in such a manner to be able to push gently away. This resistance is very important for learning to follow.

2. & 3. The man's right hand on the woman's left shoulder blade is actually two points of touch—the fingers and the heel of the hand. The fingers exert a small amount of pressure when leading a left turn and the heel exerts pressure when leading a right turn. (The man's right arm should be under the woman's left in closed position).

4. The woman's left arm touches the top of the man's right arm, but she does not rest on it. The man lifts his elbow very slightly when beginning a move forward (woman backward), or when stopping the woman's forward motion after he has been stepping backward.

5. The man's (or leader's) left hand is palm up and is comfortably to the side, slightly lower than the woman's (or follower's) shoulder. The woman places her right hand, palm down, in the man's hand, taking care to maintain support of her own arm.

Chapter 5
Leading and Following

Learning to lead and follow takes much practice and patience. The man is usually the designated leader of the movements and the woman follows. It is simply a case of the man gently giving a subtle signal with a push or a pull and the woman giving resistance. This indicates to him that she feels the signal. There are times, however, when the woman should signal to the man that he is leading too fast or the movements are too broad, or if the man is moving backward and is about to bump into someone.

It is a good idea to practice with the woman leading the movements some of the time. This gives both the man and the woman a feel for the expectations of the other. This can easily be done without changing the basic dance position. The teacher simply directs the class to dance with the woman leading, or when practicing alone, the couple can simply agree for the lead to be changed.

GUIDELINES

1. Always maintain posture, balance and weight support.

2. Hold your partner with confidence and comfort.
3. Practice moving in a confident manner. It will soon become a habit.
4. Be aware of your surroundings.

LEADING

Always keep the arms and shoulders comfortably firm and steady, especially while signaling a lead. Rarely are any of the lead indications below used alone. Each is a subtle action that only the partner can detect except in the case of extravagant figures. Practice them separately and together.

1. Move the body slightly in the desired direction at the same time the leg begins to move toward a step.
2. Move the shoulders with the body (except in a few rare cases). The leader indicates a right turn by turning the body so that the right shoulder moves slightly backward and the left forward. A left turn is indicated by doing the opposite.

Leading and Following

3. Lift the right arm from shoulder to elbow very slightly with the forward movement of the shoulders to signal a movement forward or to stop a movement backward. Lift the arm for a movement to the leader's left and lower the arm for a movement to the leader's right. These sideways movements can also be indicated by leaning in the desired direction.

   Arm movements alone indicate the direction for figures such as the arch under, especially in the swing position.

4. Press the palm of the right hand against the follower's shoulder blade to indicate that she should go forward, or to stop her backward motion. Use the heel of the right hand to indicate a right turn and the fingers to indicate a left turn.

Remember:

1. Know a movement before attempting to lead it.
2. Decide exactly what you want to lead before initiating.
3. Make the lead indication inconspicuous, but firm.
4. Try easy movements until rapport is established with your partner.
5. Have a variety of movements in mind, but do not try everything in every dance. Remember, this is fun time, not show-off time.
6. Dance with the music.
7. Dance with small steps, especially with a new partner.

8. Always maintain a comfortable amount of arm tension.

FOLLOWING

1. Maintain a comfortable firmness in the arms to create some resistance, especially in turns or pivots.
2. Try not to guess or anticipate before the signal and follow it gently.
3. Try to take a step slightly smaller than you think you need in each movement. Then, if you have misjudged, it is much easier to adjust to a larger step than a smaller one.
4. Learn a variety of movements, but if you do not understand a lead, ask.
5. When the leader is moving backward, the follower should signal with hand pressure to prevent bumping into someone (or something).

Chapter 6
Rhythm

Dance steps either go exactly with the music or fit the musical rhythm in some way. However, dance steps and music are not always counted in the same manner and understanding the difference and how they fit is important.

MUSIC

The regular pattern of accents, or beats, is easily heard in most ballroom dance music. Each tune is counted in either twos, threes, or fours beginning with the count of one on the heaviest accented beat. It is also important to remember that dance music comes in varying speeds, known as "tempo," and should be counted accordingly.

DANCE

After recognizing how to count the beats of the music, the dance student must also be able to distinguish between steps that take one-half beat of music (Quick) and steps which take twice as long or one beat of music (Slow). It is most important to think of the rhythm of the steps in a comparative perspective. A "Slow" step takes twice as long as a "Quick." These designations are used only in dances which have both. Often, dances require steps or movements between the beats. These movements are designated "and," as in "1 and 2," for half-way between beats ("Quick, Quick, Slow" if counting the dance steps); "e" for one-fourth after the beat; and "uh" for one-fourth before the beat, as in "1 e and uh 2." The "e" and the "uh" do not fit in with the Quick and Slow designations.

Dance Count: 1 3 & u 2 3 & u
Step Rhythm: S Q Q

RELATING DANCE TO MUSIC

The dance student should remember that "Quick" and "Slow" designations are related to the tempo of the music and may be a different speed with different music. This means that the "Quick" and "Slow" steps in any dance are related only to each other with the particular piece of music which is being played. Either may be slower or faster than they are when a different piece of music is playing.

There are many variations of musical rhythm for other kinds of dancing and several ways dance teachers count musical rhythm. Dance teachers often count steps or movements instead of music which may cause frustration for students who also study music, but problems can be kept to a minimum if "dance counts" are thought of as different from music counts.

Rhythm

It is often confusing for new dance students to know which dance to do with certain music. Be patient and do not be afraid to try two or three dances if you are not sure. Composers are rarely thinking about dancers when they are composing music. Even music that is recorded for specific dances does not always work. And some music is appropriate for more than one dance. Even dancers with much experience have to listen, think, and try a dance or two to some unfamiliar pieces of music. Be brave!

Chapter 7
Teaching Sequence

The dances in this book are arranged so that students will learn new basic principles in each dance which will help in the next dances. This enables students to learn the basics while concentrating on fewer ideas at a time. After learning the basics of dances in this book students should easily be able to learn other dances. The following is an explanation of the order chosen for this book.

1. **Cha-Cha** — Students learn the difference between slow and quick movements, changes of direction, and basic pivoting with little effort toward leading and following. Figures are added to this dance later in the course.

2. **Tango** — The rhythm is basically the same as the Cha-Cha. The students begin to learn leading and following in the social dance position and some basic arm figures. Stick to the basics and teach more difficult figures later in the term.

3. **Waltz** — A new musical rhythm is introduced and there are no Slows and Quicks in counting the dance rhythm. Rather, the concentration is on leading and following turns. This dance is inserted

here to take the students away from the rhythm of the Tango since its similarity to the Swing and Foxtrot rhythm can be very confusing.

4. **Merengue** — This is an introduction to the Latin style of movement in which students are encouraged to move their hips as they dance. It is simple and there is no change in step rhythm (no Slows or Quicks) and many arm figures can be introduced that will be used in other dances.

5. **Rumba (Rhumba)** — Students learn to add the hip movements learned in the Merengue to a more complex step pattern in this slow and controlled dance.

6. **Swing** — Students enjoy this dance. It is basically a variation of the Foxtrot, but in a more relaxed and peppy style. They learn the rhythm of the Foxtrot while using the arm figures from the Merengue.

7. **Foxtrot** — Since the most common Foxtrot dance rhythm crosses over the rhythm of the music, students learn to concentrate on the rhythm of the step sequence learned in the Swing. Students may also enjoy the Foxtrot variation known as Texas Two-Step.

8. **Mambo (commonly called "Salsa")** — Students like to try this challenging dance. It is fast, has arm figures similar to the ones already learned, and utilizes hip movements. The music is fast and exciting. When the Merengue or the Rumba are played fast, they are also designated as "Salsa" which means "hot."

Teaching Sequence

Note: There is more than enough movement in the dances listed above to keep even the fastest learners busy during the course, but sometimes they will request others. Easy dances to include, if time permits, are the Texas Two-Step, Cajun Two-Step, and some folksy Texas and Cajun variations of the Waltz.

9. **Cajun** — Students can now branch out into "folksy" styles of ballroom dance. Cajun dance is popular in many areas and is lots of fun. The dances have rhythm structures which have already been learned such as the Waltz, Merengue, Rumba, and Salsa.

10. **Country Western** — This is another "folksy" style which is popular in many areas. It has variations of the Waltz and the Foxtrot.

Chapter 8
Key to Abbreviations in Dance Descriptions

Bhd	Behind
Bsd	Beside
Bwd	Backward
Cl	Close, step beside the standing foot
Ct	Count
CCW	Counter clockwise
CW	Clockwise
Dg	Diagonal
Fwd	Forward
F	Foot
Hm	Home, return foot to last placement
L	Left
LOD	Line of Direction (or Dance), usually CCW around the dance floor

M	Man or Leader
Meas	Measure(s)
Pl	Place, same as "Home"
Pv	Pivot
Q	Quick, which takes one-half as much time as a Slow, and is used only when a dance sequence also has a Slow
R	Right
S	Slow, a step which lasts twice as long as a Quick; used only when a sequence has a Q
St	Step
StSq	Step Sequence, a basic pattern of steps
Sdw	Sideways
Tch	Touch the floor with the free foot
V	Variation, same figure with some different steps
W	Woman or Follower
Wt	Weight, as in "no Wt." or "Wt. on the heel"
X	Cross

Chapter 9
Cha-Cha

The Cha-Cha, as we know it, was developed by dance teachers in the United States from dance styles found in Cuba in the early part of the 20th century. The step sequence is easily learned if the student begins on the first beat of each measure as described below. Students who take their dance skills outside the classroom will soon discover that another version of the Cha-Cha is to begin the step sequence on the second beat of each dance measure. This is known as the Cuban Cha-Cha. Students are encouraged to try both versions.

The Cha-Cha is danced facing your partner in social dance position, swing position, or facing without hands joined. It is easier to begin in swing position. The man leads by guiding the woman's hands.

The Cha-Cha music rhythm is counted in fours (4:4 meter), but there are five steps in the basic sequence, Slow, Slow, Quick, Quick, Slow. Counted with the music this would be: 1, 2, 3, &, 4. The first and second sequences are listed here because they begin with the opposite foot and direction.

Note: The Cha-Cha version known as the Cuban Cha-Cha is the same as described below except that it begins on count 2 of the music, therefore ending on count 1 of the next measure.

Couples stand face to face in closed, swing, or disco position.

BASIC STEP

Dance Ct.:		1	2	3	&	4
Step Rhythm:		S	S	Q	Q	S
StSq 1:	M	L fwd	R hm	L pl	R pl	L pl
	W	R bwd	L hm	R pl	L pl	R pl
StSq 2:	M	R bwd	L hm	R pl	L pl	R pl
	W	L fwd	R hm	L pl	R pl	L pl

TRAVEL STEP

With the same step rhythm, simply continue forward or backward. This is usually taught later in the course because it is more comfortable to do in the social dance position.

CROSSOVER

The step sequence is the same as for the Basic. Even though this appears to be a crossing of the leg in front of the body, in reality the dancer merely pivots approximately 1/4 toward the standing leg and steps forward (count 1), then pivots back to face the original direction on the next step backward to home where the Quick, Quick, Slow (cha-cha-cha) steps are done in place or moving slightly sideways (Figure 9.1).

The Crossover is done the same as in the Basic sequence except on step sequence 1, the man pivots 1/4 to the right (on the left foot) before count 1 and pivots 1/4 to the left (on the right foot, to face the original direction) before count 3. The woman does just the opposite, causing both to pivot toward the same room direction and pivot back to face each other. On step sequence 2, each person reverses the action of step sequence 1 (Figure 9.2). After a few of these (any even number), the dancers can pivot completely around on the first step to face each other ending the series.

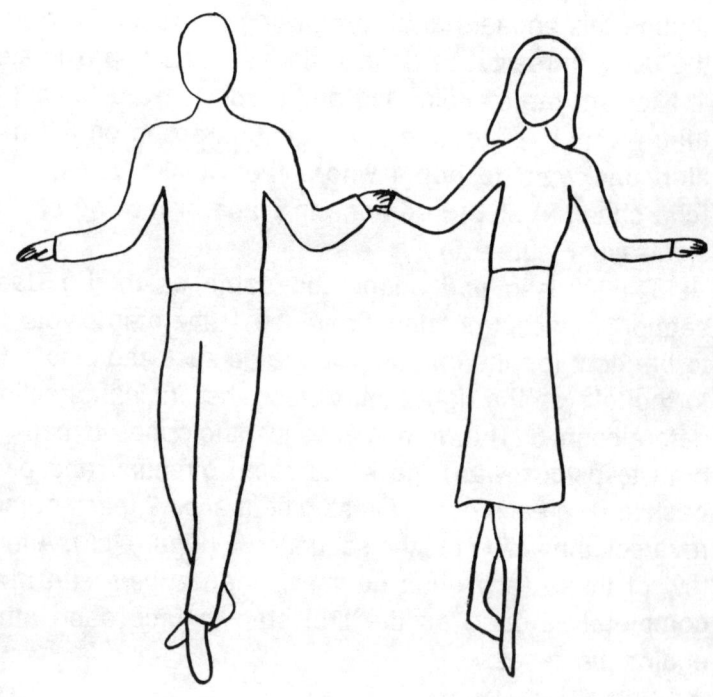

**Figure 9.1
Crossover, First Step**

Cha-Cha

**Figure 9.2
Crossover, Second Step**

HALF-TURN CHASE

The Half-Turn Chase begins in facing position. Hands are turned loose on the first step. The leader pivots 1/2 to his right on the first step forward, steps at home on the second and finishes the Basic sequence there. The follower merely observes this sequence while executing the first Basic. The second sequence is just the opposite for the leader. He steps forward with his right foot (away from his partner) and pivots 1/2 left on count 1, left home on count 2, and in place on counts 3, &, 4. Meanwhile, the follower repeats the exact movement on step sequence 2 that the leader did on step sequence 1. Partners appear to be chasing each other (Figure 9.3).

Dance Ct.:		1	&	2	3	&	4
StSq 1:	M	st L	pv R	R hm	L pl	R pl	L pl
	W	R bwd		L hm	R pl	L pl	R pl
StSq 2:	M	R bwd		L hm	R pl	L pl	R pl
	W	st L	pv R	R hm	L pl	R pl	L pl

The woman continues to turn one step sequence behind until the man stops the figure by going into a Basic step sequence after completing an even number (2, 4, 6,) of the turn sequences. The woman continues to complete one last turn sequence while the leader is doing a first Basic sequence. The follower is then ready to do a second Basic sequence at the same time as the leader.

After the man ends the figure, do step sequences 1 and 2. The woman is now facing away from the man.

Cha-Cha

Dance Ct.:		1	2	3	&	4
StSq 1:	M	L fwd	R hm	L pl	R pl	L pl
	W	st R, pv L	L hm	R pl	L pl	R pl
StSq 2:	M	R bwd	L hm	R pl	L pl	R pl
	W	L fwd	R hm	L pl	R pl	L pl

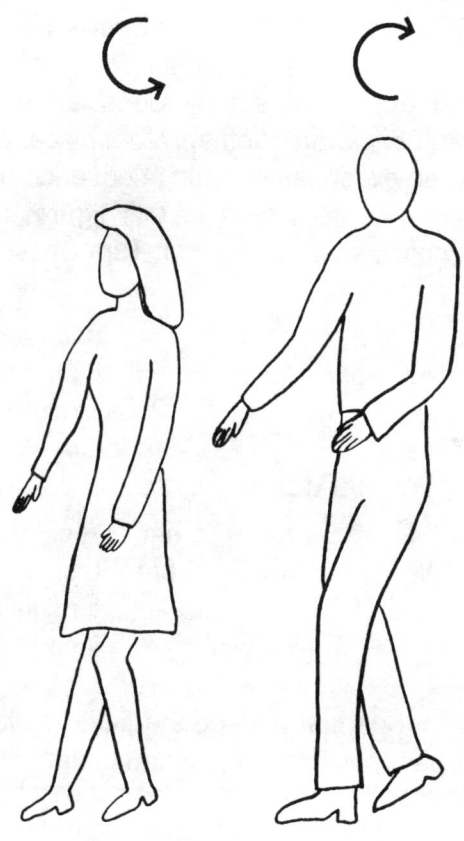

**Figure 9.3
Half-Turn Chase**

FULL-TURN CHASE

The Full-Turn Chase is actually easier to conceptualize than the Half-Turn Chase. The Full-Turn Chase begins exactly the same for the first two steps. Then, the leader completes another 1/2 turn in place while stepping counts 3, &, 4. During this, the follower does her first Basic sequence with no turns. The man does not turn on the second sequence. He simply does a second Basic sequence (left backward, home, place, place, place) while she copies the exact same turning sequence he did. Only one partner turns at a time in this figure. It does not resemble a chase as much the Half-Turn Chase.

Dance Ct.:		1	&	2	3	&	4
StSq 1:	M	st L	pv R	R hm	L pl turning 1/2 R to face W	R pl	L pl
	W	R bwd		L hm	R pl	L pl	R pl
StSq 2:	M	R bwd		L hm	R pl	L pl	R pl
	W	st L	pv R	R hm	L pl turning 1/2 R to face M	R pl	L pl

Note: Either partner may do the full turn alone holding one of their partner's hands up to turn under.

ARCH UNDER

The man lifts either arm, turning loose of the other, and leads the woman under as he steps backward on step sequence 2 of the Basic. She continues for a full turn as she did in the Full-Turn Chase (Figure 9.4). If he wishes to change places with her, he guides her to his left side as he is stepping backward on step sequence 2 of the Basic and steps around her back as she turns halfway and turns to face her on counts 3, &, 4.

BOX STEP

The Box Step works best while in closed position.

Dance Ct.:		1	2	3	&	4
StSq 1:	M	L fwd	R sdw	L pl	R pl	L pl
	W	R bwd	L sdw	R pl	L pl	R pl

StSq 2: Reverse everything.

**Figure 9.4
Arch Under**

Chapter 10
Tango
(American or Parisian)

The Tango has been through considerable evolution since it came to the United States from France in the early part of the 20th century. Popularized in Paris by refugees from Buenos Aires, its roots lie in the dances of the Gauchos. In Paris it was adapted by the upper crust of society from the Apache (Ah-Paash), a dance popular on the seedy side of town. The Tango became popular around the turn of the century due to the distribution of the music by an English recording company. The famous Ballroom dancers Irene and Vernon Castle popularized the Tango in the United States. Through the years, dance teachers have organized the steps and codified the style making the Tango what it is today. Tours by Argentine Tango dancers beginning in the late 1980s revived interest and influenced change to make the dance even more exciting. The Argentine styling and step rhythm is much more complicated.

RHYTHM AND STYLE

Tango music is usually in 4:4 meter and sometimes in 2:4. Dance students should not be concerned about the difference because it is easily counted Slow, Slow, Quick, Quick, Slow. This is the same count as the Cha-Cha, but the music is easily distinguishable. The basic step sequence has four steps and a pause. Each step sequence usually begins with the same foot. (Recent innovations are rapidly changing this.)

The dance is known for its smooth gliding style accented with quick sharp movements and pauses. It should exude quiet, explosive energy.

BASIC STEP (TANGO CLOSE)

Dance Ct.:		1	2	3	&	4
Step Rhythm:		S	S	Q	Q	S
StSq:	M	L fwd	R fwd	L sdw	R hm	tch L
	W	R bwd	L bwd	R sdw	L hm	tch R

Optional Ending with Turn Variation

Dance Ct.:	1	2	3	&	4
M	L fwd	R fwd	L fwd	R sdw	tch L
variation	L fwd	R fwd	pv L	R sdw	tch L
W	R bwd	L bwd	R bwd	L sdw	tch R
variation	R bwd	L bwd	pv L	L sdw	tch R

Tango

One of the recent fun and exciting innovations has been to occasionally substitute the Quick, Quick, Slow steps in counts 3, &, 4 for the Slow, Slow steps in counts 1, 2. This works for most of the figures. Practice this with the Basic Step to help with leading and following skills.

CORTE

This is simply an exaggerated change of direction after the first step and can be done forward or backward. Maintain some weight on the free foot for style and balance.

Dance Ct.:		1	2	3 & 4
StSq:	M	L bwd	R hm	(any of the above endings)
	W	R fwd	L hm	(any of the above endings)

The Corte is sometimes executed on the third step when the man is traveling backward in place of the Quick, Quick, Touch.

SEMI-OPEN

Made famous by the movies, dancers turn toward their outstretched arms (the man turns 1/4 to the left; the woman, 1/4 to the right) to face the same direction. Pivot to face your partner after count 2. The man's right shoulder touches the woman's left shoulder (Figure 10.1).

Dance Ct.:	1	2	3	&	4
StSq: M	L fwd	R fwd, pv R	L sdw	R hm	tch L
W	R fwd	L fwd, pv L	R sdw	L hm	tch R

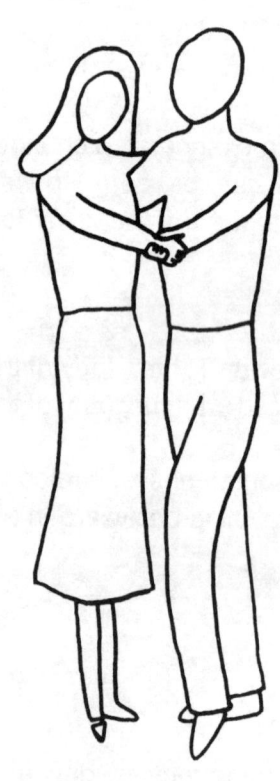

**Figure 10.1
Semi-Open**

ARCH UNDER FROM SEMI-OPEN

The man lifts his left arm and guides the woman into a full turn as he walks beside her on the first two counts. Then he adds one of the above endings.

To change places during the arch under, the man simply walks around behind the woman as both turn halfway to face, returning to closed position, in the opposite direction.

ARCH UNDER FROM CLOSED

The man steps backward and lifts his left arm as in the Corte. The woman releases her left arm and turns to her right under the uplifted arms. Then the man steps forward and around behind the woman as they change places and return to closed position or remain open for another figure.

OPEN REVERSE

Begin with a sequence in the semi-open position and on the pivot after the second step, turn 1/2 to face the opposite direction and separate to arm's length on the third step holding only the man's left hand to the woman's right hand.

From this position two easy figures can be done.

1. **Sweep** — Both partners take one step forward, pivot 1/2 toward each other, step in the original

Semi-Open direction on the second step, pivot 1/4 to Closed position and end with the Tango Close step.

2. **Arch Under** — From the open reverse position as described above or from the closed position.

CLOSED SWEEP

The man leads the woman as both pivot approximately 1/4 to each partner's left before step 1. This places them close, almost right side-by-side, facing opposite directions. On count 1, the man steps backward as in the Corte, the woman steps forward, and the woman immediately pivots 1/2 to the right to Semi-Open. Step on count 2 (and the rest of the phrase) as in the Semi-Open figure described above.

Chapter 11
Merengue

The Merengue came to the United States in the mid-1950s from the Caribbean. It is known throughout Latin America by various names and in Texas as the Mexican One-Step. It is commonly done with the Mambo and Rumba in the Salsa (hot and fast music) scene and utilizes many arm figures. It was popular in the early days to do the steps sideways while swaying the hips and keeping the following leg straight.

BASIC WALK

In closed position, the man walks forward or backward beginning with the left foot and continues stepping at a lively pace changing direction at any time and turning. The woman does the opposite footwork.

SIDEWAYS

In closed position, the man steps with the left foot to the left and closes the right foot (which is kept straight) to the left. This continues until a change of direction is desired. Dancers can move into the Basic or change feet to move sideways to the man's right. To do this the man touches the right foot instead of stepping on it and begins traveling sideways to the right. The woman does the opposite footwork.

ARCH UNDER

The man drops his right arm hold and lifts his left arm to guide the woman under for a full turn. The man can then turn under it himself or change hands and guide the woman under the other hand. From this position (swing position) any number of arm figures can be invented as long as both dancers are comfortable.

LOCK

From swing position, the woman turns under her right arm (holding the man's left hand) while continuing to hold the man's right hand (in the woman's left) at waist level as it wraps around her back (Figure 11.1). Meanwhile, the man turns 1/4 to the left to put the dancers' right shoulders toward each other. The dancers walk around each other in this position until an exit is desired.

To exit, the man can release his left hand and turn under the uplifted held hands to face the woman, or the woman can simply turn left to unwrap.

Merengue

**Figure 11.1
Lock**

PRETZEL

The hands are held for the entire figure. Practice slowly and do not force the arms.

From the Lock figure, the man moves sideways right across back to back to woman's other side while keeping the man's right arm at waist level and lifting his left arm over his head. When he gets to the other side (left to left shoulder) he lifts his left arm over the woman's head as she turns to her left to face the man. She does not turn any more. The man then turns right to face her while passing his left arm over his head. This last turn will feel strange at first because the man is turning away from his left arm as he turns under it.

Chapter 12
Waltz

The Waltz came about as an adaptation of the Austrian Leandler, which dates at least to the Middle Ages. During the Renaissance it became the Allemande, the Waltzer, then the Waltz. It was the first dance to use the closed position and dancers were severely criticized. It was the first so-called "dirty dance."

There are many styles of the Waltz. The fast stepping and turning Viennese style is probably the oldest, popularized by the music of Johann Strauss. Most Waltzes are danced in a smooth style with lots of turns while moving in a circle around the room. In the United States, the Waltz is often much slower.

RHYTHM

The music and the dance are counted in threes (3:4 meter) with an accent on the first beat. There are no Slow or Quick steps in the ordinary Waltz. Each step takes the same amount of time. The designation is simply, Step, Step, Step. The first step of each three, however, usually covers more distance.

WALTZ BALANCE

This is the basic forward and backward step sequence. In closed position, the man steps forward on count 1 and in place for counts 2 and 3 anticipating a backward motion during all three steps. Then he steps backward in the same fashion. The woman does the opposite motion.

Dance Ct.:		1	2	3
StSq:	M	L fwd	R pl	L pl
	W	R bwd	L pl	R pl

Repeat in the opposite direction with the opposite foot. It can also be done from side to side.

TRAVELING WALTZ

The Traveling Waltz is almost like walking with a longer step on the first of each three steps with a feeling similar to the Waltz Balance. The man usually goes forward; the woman backward, in closed position. A variation is for both to go forward in semi-open position and turn to face the partner in closed position at the end of a second step sequence.

BOX STEP AND COUNTER-CLOCKWISE TURNS

The Waltz Box step is used most often for revolving counter-clockwise and traveling around the floor. With practice, dancers can learn to turn halfway around with each step sequence. If this is continued, the dancers will travel. The travel sequence should begin with the man facing in the line of direction (Figure 12.1).

Dance Ct.:		1	2	3
StSq:	M	L fwd	R sdw	L pl (cl and change wt)
	W	R bwd	L sdw	R pl (cl and change wt)

This is half of the box. Repeat the steps in the opposite direction with the opposite foot on the next step sequence to complete it. To do the Box Turn, begin turning left as the leg reaches out for the first step. Continue to revolve during the next two steps (Figure 12.2).

The man should think of turning the left toe out as he steps forward on the first count of step sequence 1 and turn the right toe in as he steps backward on the first count of step sequence 2. The woman does just the opposite.

It is important to turn the shoulders so that the body is facing the same direction as the toe of the reaching foot (cue: "the nose and toes point in the same direction").

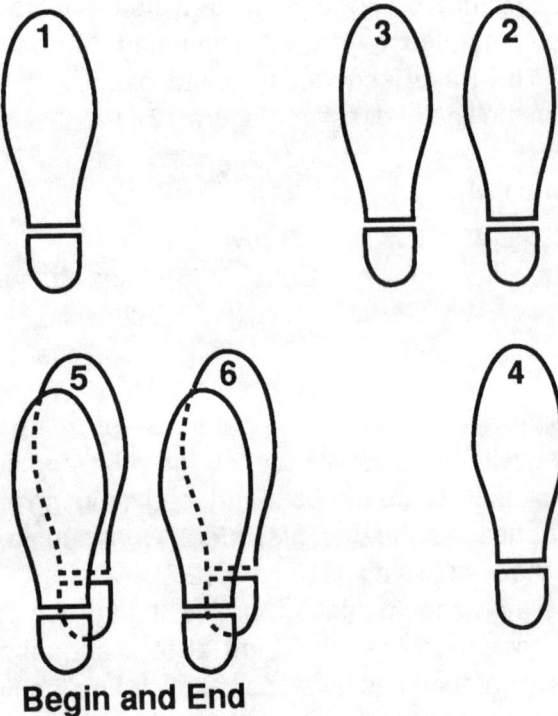

**Figure 12.1
Waltz Box Step**

Waltz 53

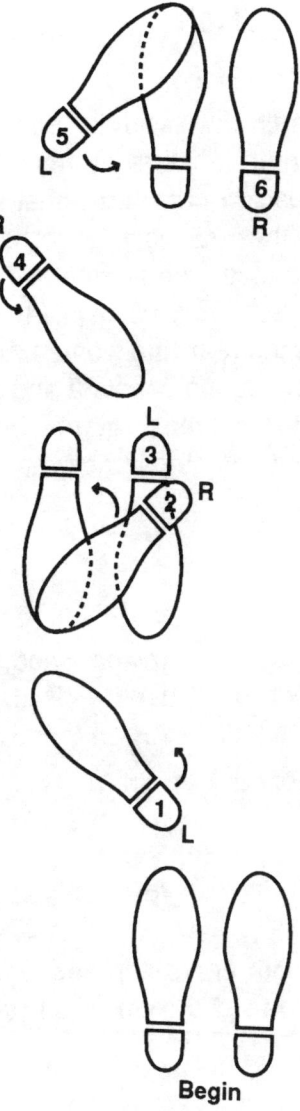

**Figure 12.2
Counter-Clockwise Turn**

BACK-STEP TURN

This turn goes clockwise and requires small steps. It works best if the man faces away from the center of the room in closed position. The turn must begin before the first step so that the man is facing the reverse line of direction before he takes the first step. The man's left leg actually begins by reaching sideways, but the man turns so that he will step to the rear (the woman's right foot forward R). Continue turning during counts 2 and 3 so that 1/2 turn is completed in three steps. At the beginning of step sequence 2, the woman steps backward with her left foot on count 1.

Dance Ct.:		1	2	3
StSq 1:	M	L bwd	R pl	L pl
			(pv on 2 and 3)	
	W	R fwd	L pl	R pl
			(pv on 2 and 3)	
StSq 2:	M	R fwd	L pl	R pl
			(pv on 2 and 3)	
	W	L bwd	R pl	L pl
			(pv on 2 and 3)	

Turn halfway with each step sequence, continuing in the same direction to complete a full turn by the end of step sequence 2.

Waltz

BOX TURN/SIDE-TURN COMBINATION

The Box Turn/Side-Turn combination is recommended for Level 2 students.

To learn this figure, students should do four of each combination. Begin with the Box turn facing the line of direction, but complete only 1/4 turn during the second (last) step sequence 2. This will place the man facing away from the center of the room in a position to begin the Back-Step turn. End this series of four in the same manner by turning only 1/4 during the second (last) step sequence 2. End with the man facing the line of direction. Begin the Box Turn again.

TRAVELING CROSS STEP

This is a traveling step which goes in a zig-zag path. The first step of each step sequence appears to cross the body as the dancers pivot approximately 1/8 before stepping.

Dance Ct.:		1	2	3
StSq 1:	M	L fwd	R sdw (turn 1/8 L)	L pl
	W	R bwd	L bwd (turn 1/8 R)	R pl
StSq 2:	(M st 1, X in front of W, W st 1, X bhd)			
	M	R fwd X	L sdw (turn 1/8 L)	R pl
	W	L bwd X	R sdw (turn 1/8 R)	L pl

Repeat with the opposite foot and direction, traveling in the line of direction.

End by beginning a Box Step turn at the end of any step sequence 2.

Chapter 13
Swing

The Swing dance is a variation of the Foxtrot. Music for the Foxtrot tends to be slow and romantic, while Swing dance music is faster and has more pep. True Swing music has a stress on the upbeat, but some music is played in a way that either dance style can be done.

Swing dancing has many names: Lindy, Jitterbug, Boogie, East Coast, West Coast, and Shag. In the 1930s, the style came into its glory with the popularity of "Swing" music even though it evolved from the African American dance style known as Jazz which was popular in New York's Harlem district.

The name, Swing, most probably came from the idea of swinging out away from your partner and turning under each other's arms. The name "Jitterbug" seems to have begun with a New York newspaper reporter describing the acrobatic moves. However, the heavy-on-the-upbeat music style which went with the dance was also known as "Swing." It has many, many styles and variations of step sequence throughout the U.S. and has evolved likewise in other countries. It can be slow or fast.

RHYTHM AND STYLE

Swing and Foxtrot music is counted in either two (2:4 meter) or four (4:4 meter) beats per measure. There is a variety of step rhythms for either dance. However, the most common Foxtrot step rhythm, Slow, Slow, Quick, Quick, was popularized and named the "Murray Magic Rhythm" by dance school founder Arthur Murray and is the basis for the most common Swing style also known as the Single Lindy.

Each step sequence is easily counted 1, 2, 3, & which makes it cross over the music. This means that the first and every odd numbered step sequence will end in the middle of a phrase or a measure. This may cause some initial confusion, but most Swing and Foxtrot music is easy to follow.

2:4 Music:	1	2	1	2	1	2	1	2
4:4 Music:	1	2	3	4	1	2	3	4
Dance Ct.:	1	2	3	&	1	2	3	&
Step Rhythm:	S	S	Q	Q	S	S	Q	Q
M	L	R	L	R	L	R	L	R
W	R	L	R	L	R	L	R	L

POSITION

Partners face each other, holding hands; or begin in social dance position and hold hands after the first turn (Figure 13.1).

**Figure 13.1
Swing Position**

BASIC SWING STEP

The music is a 2:4 (sometimes 4:4) meter.
The dance counts are: 1, 2, 3, &. (Yes, it feels like it does not go with the music).

Dance Ct.:		1	2	3	&
StSq:	M	L pl	R pl	L bhd	R hm
	W	R pl	L pl	R bhd	L hm

ARM FIGURES

All arm figures are executed on the first two steps.

Arch Under and Return

The man leads the arch under by raising his left hand (which hold the woman's right hand) before count 1, so the woman can turn to her right on count 1. The man must turn loose of the other hand. The man can either stand in place or travel behind her (changing places with her) at the same time (Figure 13.2a).

Both dancers step backward (count 3) and step in place (count &) before reversing the turn going back to the original spot on the next step sequence.

These turns can be done in any sequence and with either hand. Options include holding both hands up during the two turns or holding none. If holding none, the man must give a firm indication of the lead (see Woman Turn Alone, below).

Swing

Note: The two basic turns executed in the figure above are the basis for most figures.

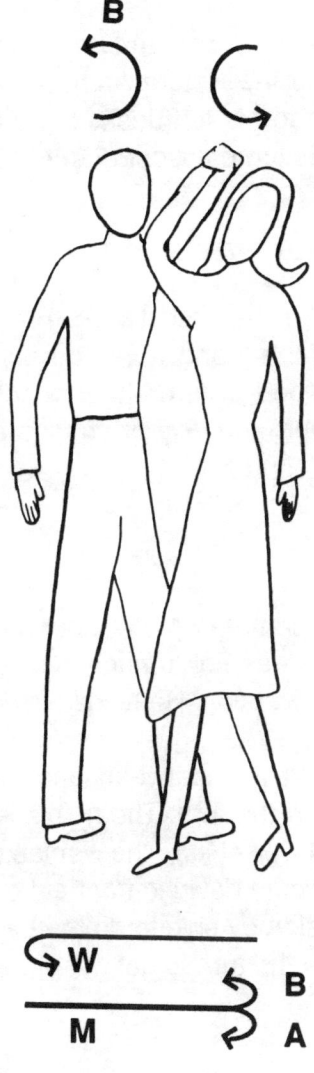

Figure 13.2
Arch Under Return (A) and Double Arch Under (B)

Double Arch Under

Both the man and the woman turn under the arch. This step is the same as the Return Arch (see above) except that the man turns to his left under the arms on count 2 after the woman has turned under (Figure 13.2b).

Woman Turn Alone

This begins like the arch figure, but the man turns loose of the woman's hand after the initial guide. The woman can be guided to turn either way by either hand and be guided to turn in place or change places with the man.

Woman Wrap

The turn is the same as Arch Under, but the arms are different. The man does not turn loose of either hand and does not turn his own body. He holds his right hand up as the woman turns 1/2 to her right (away from her uplifted left hand). The hand travels between and in front of each partner's face during the turn. The man's left hand is held out to his left about waist high. The woman turns into it and the upheld hands come down in front of her. Both dancers are now standing side by side to do the back step (counts 3, &). Then reverse the turn to get out of the figure (Figure 13.3).

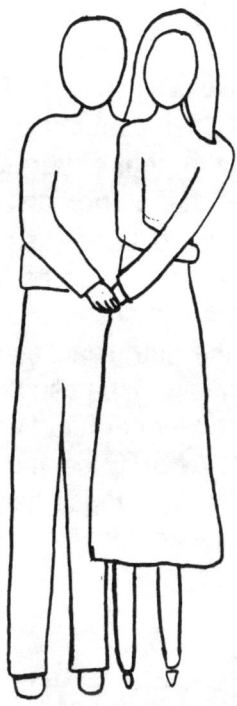

**Figure 13.3
Woman Wrap**

Man Wrap

The woman does not turn. The man holds both hands and turns 1/2 to his own left (count 1) under his own right (woman's left arm) ending to the woman's right side. Both partners do the back step and the man reverses the move on the next step sequence to exit.

Man Brush Off

The man and woman turn the same direction as in the Arch Under except the man turns loose of the woman's left hand as he passes in front of her, turning his back to her and holding his left hand (woman's right) low across his waist as he turns toward it and she passes behind him. He drops it on count 2, she slides her right hand around his back and he catches it after the turn is completed.

Variation: If the man reaches for the woman's right with his right after the turn, he can then guide her into a left turn, lifting his right over her head while he turns left into a back to back pass. As he turns and passes, he lowers his right hand behind and changes her right hand to his left. The turn should now be complete and dancers are facing each other.

STEP SEQUENCE VARIATIONS

There are several step variations that have an extra foot movement on each of the first two counts. This requires the dancer to either step quicker or dance to slower music. Arm figures are the same.

Swing

Double Lindy

M Dance Ct.:
- 1   st L in pl
- &   tch R bsd L
- 2   R hm
- &   tch L bsd R
- 3   L bwd
- &   R hm

W does opposite footwork

BeBop

M Dance Ct.:
- 1   tch ball of L in pl (body rises)
- &   L (body returns to normal)
- 2   tch ball of R in pl (body rises)
- &   R (body returns to normal)
- 3   L bwd
- &   R hm

W does opposite footwork

Triple Lindy

M Dance Ct.:
- 1   L pl
- e   R bsd L
- &   L pl
- 2   R hm
- e   L bsd R
- &   R pl
- 3   L bwd
- &   R hm

W does opposite footwork

North Carolina Shag

The North Carolina Shag combines the Single and Triple rhythms.

M Dance Ct.:
- 1   L pl
- &   circle R out and to the rear of L
- 2   R bhd L
- e   L pl
- &   R bhd L
- 3   kick L fwd (small)
- e   L bwd
- &   R hm

W does opposite footwork

Counts 3, e, & of this variation are called the "Baltimore Kick" and can be used in place of counts 3 and 3, & in any of the above Swing styles.

Chapter 14
Foxtrot

The Foxtrot got its name from a Vaudeville stage performer, Harry Fox, in the United States in the second decade of this century. His dance was a simple and spontaneous trot around the stage to ragtime music. The dance, now called the Foxtrot, has little in common with what he did. Both the dance and the music have changed many times through the years.

As mentioned in the Swing chapter, Foxtrot music is counted in either two (2:4 meter) or four (4:4 meter) beats per measure and there is a variety of step rhythms. Almost any combination of Slow and Quick steps are used by practiced dancers. However, the most common Foxtrot step rhythm, Slow, Slow, Quick, Quick, is the same as the Swing rhythm described in Chapter 13. It was popularized and named the "Murray Magic Step" by dance school founder Arthur Murray. The name and the step sequence are taught widely.

MURRAY MAGIC STEP

2:4 Music:	1	2	1	2	1	2	1	2
4:4 Music:	1	2	3	4	1	2	3	4
Dance Ct.:	1	2	3	&	1	2	3	&
Step Rhythm:	S	S	Q	Q	S	S	Q	Q
StSq: M	L	R	L	R	L	R	L	R
W	R	L	R	L	R	L	R	L

The direction can be changed on any step or turns can be done with a small pivot on the free foot.

ARCH UNDER

The man releases his right hand from the woman's back, lifts his left arm, and guides her into either a half turn as he walks around her back, or a full turn as he steps beside her. This can be done on either the first or third step as the woman is about to step on her right.

Note: The only difference in this from the Swing version is in speed and style. The dancer should exhibit an elegant and smooth, sophisticated style by using small steps in the Foxtrot.

SEMI-OPEN

Turn to face semi-open position on the first two (Slow) steps. Pivot on the second step to face each other for a side-close on the last two (Quick) steps.

Dance Ct.:		1	2	3	&
StSq:	M	L fwd	R fwd, pv R	L sdw	R cl
	W	R bwd	L bwd, pv R	R sdw	L cl

CLOCKWISE TURN AS MAN TRAVELS FORWARD

Remain in social dance position throughout the figure. The man travels forward (the woman travels backward), pivoting to his right on the second step. This guides the woman into a pivot right. The man then takes a side step left while continuing his turn to end in front of the woman, guiding the woman to do a short side step to her right. After some practice, the couple will be able to turn 1/2. Then practice the next figure during the next step sequence. The result will be a feeling of rolling one way, then the other.

Dance Ct.:		1	2	3	&
StSq:	M	L fwd	R fwd, pv R	L sdw	R cl
	W	R bwd	L bwd, pv R	R sdw	L cl

COUNTER-CLOCKWISE TURN AS MAN TRAVELS BACKWARD

Remain in social dance position throughout the figure. The man travels backward, pivoting to his left on the second step. This guides the woman into a left pivot. The man then takes a short side step left, guiding the woman to do a longer side step to her right. After some practice, the couple will be able to turn 1/2.

Dance Ct.:		1	2	3	&
StSq:	M	L bwd	R bwd, pv L	L sdw	R cl
	W	R fwd	L fwd, pv L	R sdw	L cl

ZIG-ZAG

Begin in social dance position. The man travels forward on step one, shifting his position to his left and extending his right arm to the right so that the woman's right shoulder faces the man's right shoulder. He pivots 1/2 to his right in place on the second step, guiding the woman into a 1/2 pivot right in place. This positions the couple so that their left shoulders face each other. The man's left arm is extended. The man takes two back steps (Quick, Quick) while the woman takes two forward steps. This ends step sequence one. Reverse the process on the second step sequence to return to the beginning position. Repeat these two sequences several times for the zig-zag effect.

Dance Ct.:		1	2	3	&
StSq:	M	L fwd	R fwd, pv R	L bwd	R bwd
	W	R bwd	L bwd, pv R	R fwd	L fwd

Chapter 15
Rumba (Rhumba)

This fascinating Cuban dance became popular in the U.S. during the 1930s. It blends elements of both African and Spanish dance. The movement of the hips appears African and the stately posture appears Spanish.

The basic step sequence of the Rumba had been done in the context of the Tango earlier, but the styling and the music for the two dances are unmistakably different. The Rumba is Cuba's national dance, but the U.S. version has taken on a slow and romantic style of its own. The faster Cuban style has been adopted by dancers who are Salsa music enthusiasts; and in that setting, the Rumba is often confused with the Mambo. This is not important, however, because the step rhythms of either dance go with the Salsa music.

One of the popular versions of the Cajun Two-Step (described in Chapter 18) is a fast Rumba.

RHYTHM AND STYLE

The music is in 4:4 time and the basic dance sequence has three steps. The first step takes two counts and the step rhythm is Slow, Quick, Quick. The hip movement style is the same as the Merengue. The knee is bent over the stepping foot allowing the hips to sway over the weight-bearing foot. That is, when the dancer is stepping to the left foot, the left knee is bent and the hip sways to the right side.

Dance Ct.:		1	2	3	4
Step Rhythm:		S		Q	Q
StSq:	M	L		R	L
	W	R		L	R

CLOSED POSITION

Walk

Dance Ct.:		1	2	3	4
StSq:	M	L fwd		R fwd	L fwd
	W	R bwd		L bwd	R bwd

Box

The Box step takes two step sequences to complete.

Dance Ct.:		1	2	3	4
StSq 1:	M	L fwd		R to R	L cl
	W	R bwd		L to L	R cl
StSq 2:	M	R bwd		L to L	R cl
	W	L fwd		R to R	L cl

SEMI-OPEN WALK

In semi-open position, both partners do the Walk step forward and close at the end of any second step sequence.

ARCH UNDER

The Arch Under is done exactly as in the Foxtrot from either closed or semi-open position. The man releases his right hand, lifts his left hand and guides the woman under it. He then has at least four choices: he can either do the first step sequence of Box, travel beside her, circle behind her, or go under the same uplifted arm (after her) to face her and close at the end of any second step sequence.

ESCORT

The man changes hands after the woman's Arch Under, holding her right hand with his right at his right hip as she circles clockwise behind him to arrive at his left side (Figure 15.1). She then places her left hand in his outstretched left hand. The couple is now side by side with her right hand behind his back and his left hand in front of her.

The man exits by releasing his right hand and turning the woman 1/2 turn clockwise on step sequence 1 to arrive in front of him, or turning her counter-clockwise (away from him) and under his uplifted left arm on step sequence 2 to arrive in front. As the woman arrives in front, release the hands and resume closed position.

**Figure 15.1
Escort**

Chapter 16
Samba

The Samba was developed into a ballroom dance by U.S. dance teachers based on a traditional dance from Brazil. It was first recorded in the U.S. at the 1939 New York World Fair. The music became very popular and many new tunes were written in the Samba rhythm. The U.S. style of the dance is done with an up and down motion of the knees (bouncing) while stepping forward and backward. The music is 2:4; the step sequence is made of three steps. Note that the second step is not midway between the first and third steps, but is done very close to the third step.

Dance Ct.:	1	&	u	2	1	&	u	2
Step Rhythm:	S		Q	Q	S		Q	Q
StSq: M	L		R	L	R		L	R
W	R		L	R	L		R	L

Note: Few arm figures are done with the Samba, but several listed with other dances in previous chapters are possible.

BASIC STEP SEQUENCE

Dance Ct.:		1	&	u	2	1	&	u	2
StSq:	M	fwd	cl	cl	bwd		cl	cl	
	W	bwd	cl	cl	fwd		cl	cl	

Bend the knees on counts 1 and 2, straighten on u.
Reverse the steps and direction to complete the pattern.

SEMI-OPEN

Dancers turn and face the same direction. Travel with the step, close, close in the rhythm listed above. Close at the end of any number of Basic step sequence.

SIDE STEP

Changing the step pattern to the Merengue single step, travel to the side with a step-close and return as described in the Merengue above.

DISCO

Face your partner with no hold and occasionally turn away and travel around your partner.

Chapter 17
Mambo (Salsa)

The Mambo is the dance from which the Cha-Cha evolved. It is basically a Cha-Cha with the three steps at the end dropped in favor of a single step and is done much faster. Also, done properly, it begins on the second musical beat as does the so-called "Cuban" Cha-Cha. However, the beginner should not be overly concerned with this feature and begin when the beat of the music feels right. If confused, observe experienced dancers.

Music may be either a 2:4 or 4:4 meter.

Dance Ct.:		1	&	2	&
Step Rhythm:			Q	Q	S
StSq 1:	M		L fwd	R hm	cl
	W		R bwd	L hm	cl
StSq 2:	M		R bwd	L hm	cl
	W		L fwd	R hm	cl

SIDE STEP

Dance Ct.:		1	&	2	&
StSq:	**M**	L to L	R hm	cl	
	W	R to R	L hm	cl	
StSq 2:	**M**	R to R	L hm	cl	
	W	L to L	R hm	cl	

Refer to Chapter 9, Cha-Cha, for additional figures.

STYLE NOTES

While doing the basic step sequence, try to keep the body at home. Straighten the stepping leg and keep the standing leg slightly bent on step one. The feet step away from the body on step one. While doing other figures, keep the steps small and add style by keeping the knees close to each other. This will add a small twist to the lower body. Let the hips move and sway comfortably.

Chapter 18
Cajun Dance

The word "Cajun" comes from the word "Acadian" which refers to the land from which the French-speaking settlers came to Louisiana in the 18th century. Few, if any, people exist that have a clear lineage from those original settlers, but many people who live in southwestern Louisiana and southern Texas rightfully claim the Cajun culture as their own. Cajun culture has been heavily influenced by settlers from many places and times and the dances are variations of dances that have been popular throughout the United States.

There are three basic dances popular now: the Two-Step, the Waltz, and a modern version of the Jitterbug. The Two-Step and the Waltz, which are older, are found in several rhythmic and stylistic variations. A few of those variations are listed below. (Refer to *Dance of the Cajuns* by Jerry Duke for a full discussion of the Two-Step and Waltz.)

The Black Creole cousin of Cajun music and dance is "Zydeco." Even though it recently took on the name "Zydeco," it is at least as old as if not older than Cajun and has influenced many Cajun musicians. Both are influenced by Caribbean music and dance which also has African roots with French influence. The "Two-Step" is done to both styles of music, but has a hip-swinging flair when done by black Creoles to Zydeco music.

CAJUN TWO-STEP

The Cajun Two-Step is a three step dance done to 2:4 music and is found in two rhythmic variations: Quick, Quick, Slow, and Slow, Quick, Quick. The latter is more common. The dances listed below are styles of that rhythmic variation. The "Basic" is so named because it is the more simple of the variations. It is common around Lafayette and the central part of Louisiana, but is not the only variation to be found there. All variations of the "Two-Step" are done in relaxed ballroom dance hold. The man begins with the left foot, the woman begins with the right. This alternates with each measure.

Basic

The dance rhythm is Slow, Quick, Quick.

Meas. 1:
Dance Ct.: 1 Step in place (man's left; woman's right)
& Hold
2 Step to rear (little or no turn of the body)
& Step in original place

Turn slowly in either direction. Begin the next measure on the opposite foot.

Cajun Dance

The numbers in the foot pattern illustration indicate the dance counts for two measures of 2:4 music (Figure 18.1). There is no foot movement on counts 2 and 6. Both feet can be in place with most of the weight on the foot indicated on the previous count.

```
2:4   Music counts:   1  &  2  &  1  &  2  &
      Dance counts:   1  2  3  4  5  6  7  8
```

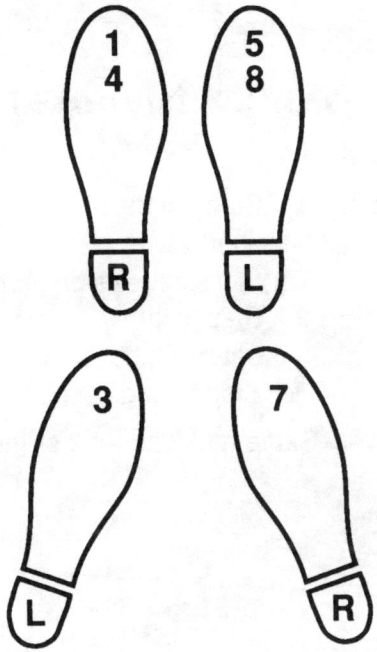

**Figure 18.1
Cajun Two-Step, Basic Step**

Basic with Travel

Moving as a couple, one partner steps forward, the other backward.

Meas. 1:
Dance Ct.: 1 Small forward (or backward) step
                   & Hold
                   2 Large step in same direction
                   & Small step in opposite direction
Meas. 2: Begin with the opposite foot.

Lake Charles (Louisiana) #1

Meas. 1:
Dance Ct.: 1 Step in place (man's left; woman's right)
                   & Slip sideways on same foot
                   2 Step slightly to side on ball of foot (man's right; woman's left)
                   & Step in original place.
Meas. 2: Same as Measure 2 of the "Basic."

Lake Charles #2

Meas. 1:
Dance Ct.: 1 Stamp in place (man's left; woman's right)
                   & Step in place with the same foot
                   2 Step either to the side or to the rear
                   & Step in original place

Meas. 2: Same as Measure 2 of the "Basic."

Lake Charles #3

Meas. 1: Same as the "Basic" or "Lake Charles #1" or "#2" (your choice)

Meas. 2:
Dance Ct.: 1 Step in place (man's right, woman's left)
                   & Hold
                   2 Step to rear while bring heel of free foot sharply across top of foot
                   & Step in original place

Zydeco (Creole)

The Zydeco is performed the same as any of the above figures with the addition of hip action sideways away from each step.

ARM FIGURES

When figures are done with the "Basic" or the "Port Arthur" styles, the dance is called "Jitterbug." However, there is a different and newer "Cajun Jitterbug" (explained later) that is popular especially among the younger dancers. Figures start on count 1, finish by count 2 and are followed by the steps found in "Basic" count 2 and count &. Figures are done from the double hand-hold position (couple is facing, holding hands) except for the "Outside Arch Under," which is also done from the ballroom position.

Outside Arch Under

The Outside Arch Under can be done on count 1 of any measure, but usually on measure 1.

The man leads the woman under his uplifted left arm, holding her right hand. She steps forward and turns to her right to face him while he steps forward and turns to his left to face her. Both turn approximately one-half. Refer to Figure 13.2 in the "Swing" chapter.

Inside Arch Under

The Inside Arch Under is most often done on measure 2 following an "Outside Arch Under" on measure 1. However, it can be done alone on count 1 of any measure. The man leads the woman across in front of him with his uplifted left arm holding her right hand. She steps forward and turns to her left to face him as he steps forward and turns to his right to face her.

Brush-Off

The Brush-Off is more easily done on measure 1, count 1. It is usually executed from the double hand-hold position. Bringing his left arm across in front of him about waist high, the man leads the woman to his right side while stepping forward and turning left away from her, releasing her. He continues to turn to face her as she turns either direction to face him (the man usually guides her turn direction).

CAJUN WALTZ

There are many ways to do a Cajun Waltz. Some variations include:

- maintaining the three count Waltz rhythm
- using four counts against the three-count music
- using four steps over two measures (two steps of which take two counts each and two take one count).

All variations are done in relaxed ballroom dance position. Below are three favorite variations.

Drive the Woman

The man begins with the left foot; the woman with the right. Step on each beat with the woman going backward and the man going forward.

This Waltz is also done by Country-Western and cowboy dancers in other parts of the country to Country-Western Waltz music.

Meas. 1:
Dance Ct.:   1 Big step
               2 Short step
               3 Short step
Meas. 2:   Opposite footwork.

The man always travels forward. He turns the woman one full turn to her right in three steps under his uplifted left arm on measure 1 (or any measure she begins with her right) foot whenever he wishes.

Cajun Cowboy Waltz

The Cajun Cowboy Waltz has a peculiar big step on the second beat. In ballroom position, the man begins with the left foot; the woman with the right. It can be done either in place or traveling.

Dance generally in one place, but turn in either direction on any measure.

Meas. 1:
Dance Ct.:   1 Step in place
               2 Step to the rear (little or no turning of the body, but dancers are stepping away from each other)
               3 Step in original place
Meas. 2:   Opposite footwork.

To travel with the Cajun Cowboy Waltz:

Meas. 1:
Dance Ct.: 1 Short step forward (the man steps forward most of time; the woman goes backward)
2 Big step in same direction
3 Short step backward (the woman steps forward when she is traveling backward)
Meas. 2 Opposite footwork.

Dance the "in place" for any number of measures. The man changes to the "travel" by changing the direction of his count 2 step from backward to forward. The woman is basically doing the same steps for "in place" as she is while "traveling" backward except for the longer steps. Count 3 does not return to the original place in the "travel" as it does in the "in place." Even though it is directed away from the direction of travel, it progresses from the original place. On those rare occasions when the man wishes the woman to go forward, he leads her into a forward step on count 2 while he takes a longer back step.

Six-Count Waltz

There are several variations of the six-count waltz found throughout Acadiana. It utilizes four steps in two measures and is really the Texas Two-Step (a popular country Western dance done in six counts to 2:4 music, using one and one-half measures) transposed to two measures of Waltz music.

The man travels forward most of the time while the woman travels backward. Occasionally the dancers turn one-half while traveling and the man goes backward for a while. In ballroom position, the man begins with the left foot; the woman begins with the right. A favorite variation is below.

Meas. 1:
Dance Ct.: 1 Touch (the man slightly forward with the left foot; the woman backward with the right)
2 Step in that spot
3 Touch in same direction with the other foot

Meas. 2:
Dance Ct.: 1 Step in that spot
2 Step in same direction
3 Step in same direction

Repeat from the beginning.

CAJUN JITTERBUG

This newer version of the "Cajun Jitterbug" has become popular in recent years at most Cajun dance events. The older dancers often do not like it because it has many fast turns, takes up more dance space, and can be hazardous to those dancing nearby. This dance was observed in a Country-Western dance hall in Arizona some 15 years ago done to Country-Western music and called the "Pony."

It is done with a simple push step (buzz step) on either foot throughout the dance, changing feet from time to time at the dancer's whim. The push is most often done on the downbeat of the music (counts 1 and 2) and the step follows on the upbeat (count &). The dance has many figures which are often continually executed. There is, however, a basic step to dance in place and a basic hold to use while traveling about the floor. The dance is done in the double hand-hold position.

Basic

Dance Ct.: 1 The man steps forward on the ball of the foot; the woman steps backward
& Both step full foot in the original place
2 The man steps backward on the ball of the foot; the woman steps forward
& Both step full foot in the original place

Continue as long as you wish. The dancers should only turn slightly in the direction of the steps, not move their centers of balance back and forth (Figure 18.2).

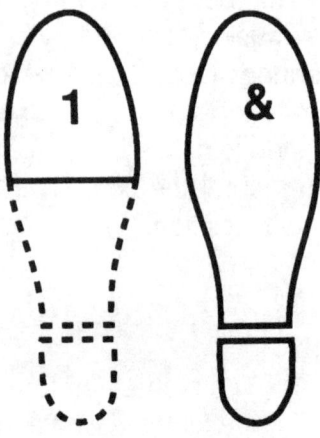

**Figure 18.2
Cajun Jitterbug, Basic Step**

Travel

This figure is done in the Varsouvienne position and begins the dance as often as the Basic (above). If dancers begin with the Basic, the man turns the lady into Varsouvienne position by taking the woman's right hand with his right, extending it to his right side (shoulder high) thus guiding the woman into a half turn to be at his right side facing the same direction. He maintains the hold on her right hand just above her shoulder and takes her left hand in front with his left hand. This action is done at any comfortable speed.

Dance Ct.:	1	Both step in place, or slightly forward, on the ball of the foot
	&	Both step forward on the full foot

Repeat for as long as you wish.

ARM FIGURES

There are many figures done with this dance. Here are a few easy, but fancy ones. The "Arch" figures and the "Brush-Off" are done as in the "Two-Step," but the speed of execution varies as the dancers wish.

Wrap and Exit

From the double hand-hold, the man extends his right arm to the right side while bring his left arm across his body leading the woman under it into a half-turn to end at his right side. Her left arm will be extended across the front of her body and remain connected to his right arm which is behind her. The woman's right arm will extend across and slightly to the front of her body above her left arm and will remain connected to his left. To exit, reverse the action. To cuddle to the man's left, do all of the actions with the opposite arm. Refer to Figure 13.2 in the "Swing" chapter.

Pretzel

This figure is divided into five parts to make it easy to follow:

1. Execute the "Wrap and Exit" to the man's left side.

2. The man continues to hold his right arm up (after the woman has turned under it to exit) and guides her into an additional full turn to her left in place without stopping. She has remained at the man's left side. She will now be standing at his left side facing the opposite direction. Her right arm is extended behind her, holding the man's left (which is extended to his left side). Her left arm is extended to her left side, in front of the man, continuing to hold his right hand which is about chest high in front of him.

3. The man guides the woman behind him by bringing his right hand over his head. The man and woman are now back to back, still holding hands.

4. The man turns the woman to her right by moving his right arm over her head as he turns slightly to his right and looks at her over his right shoulder. *(Be careful, the man must watch his elbow or it will strike the woman's face.)*

5. The man moves his right arm over his own head as he turns to his left to face the woman.

The partners should now be facing each other in the double hand-hold position in which they started. The five parts of this figure should be executed smoothly and at a comfortable speed. With considerable practice it can be done rather fast.

Zydeco Shuffle

Also known as the "Harlem Shuffle" among Zydeco music fans, this dance appears to be a variation of the Country-Western dance known as the "Tush-Push."

It is done to 4:4 Zydeco music (which sounds like "Rock and Roll"). Dancers stand in one or more lines side-by-side, not touching, and all facing the same direction.

Meas. 1:
Dance Ct.:
1 Step left to left
2 Step right behind left traveling left
3 Step left to left
4 Pause

Meas. 2: Repeat to the right with opposite footwork

Meas. 3:
Dance Ct.:
1 Step left forward
2 Close right to left
3 Step left forward
4 Pause

Meas. 4:
Dance Ct.:
1 Step left forward while shifting the hips forward and keeping the right foot in place
2 Reverse that action
3 Repeat count 1
& Repeat count 2
4 Repeat count 1, lifting the right foot to the left calf and turning 1/4 to the left
& Step right in place

Begin the dance again, facing the new direction.

Chapter 19
Country-Western Dance

TEXAS TWO-STEP

The Texas Two-Step is a variation of the Foxtrot and is done in a modified ballroom (closed) position (the man faces the line of direction, the woman faces to the right of the line of direction). The man holds the woman's right hand with his left, extended to his left and slightly forward. His right hand is on top of her left shoulder and serves as the main guide for the dance. Her left hand is either drooped over his right elbow (her elbow hanging down), or, when familiar, her left thumb is hooked into his right belt loop.

The basic sequence of the dance has four steps: the first two are done in one-half the time as the last two (count 1, &, 2, 3, 4, or Quick, Quick, Slow, Slow). This feels a bit awkward at first because it takes three measures of 2:4 music or, less common, one and one-half measures of 4:4. The directions below are written for 2:4 music. Unless otherwise specified, all figures are broken down into segments which take the first three steps of one basic sequence.

Basic Sequence

Instructions for the Basic Sequence are for two sequences for clarity.

Meas. 1:
Dance Ct.: 1 The man steps forward with his left foot; the woman steps backward with her right
              & The man steps forward with his right foot; the woman steps backward with her left (short steps)
              2 Repeat count 1

Meas. 2:
Dance Ct.: 1 The man steps forward with his right foot; the woman steps backward with her left (same as measure 1, count &, with a normal step)
              2 Begin the sequence again by repeating measure 1, count 1
              & Repeat measure 1, count &

Meas. 3:
Dance Ct.: 1 Repeat measure 1, count 1
              2 Repeat measure 2, count 1

These sequences can be repeated as the couple travels around the room counter-clockwise as long as desired.

Couple 1/2 Turn Clockwise

Meas. 1: As above (or any first three steps of the basic sequence by applying directions to the appropriate counts)

Meas. 2:
Dance Ct.:
1. (or the last step of a basic sequence) The man leads a 1/4 clockwise turn as the couple pivots
& The man steps to the left with his left foot to complete a 1/2 turn; the woman steps with her right foot in place (the man now faces to the right of the line of direction; the woman faces the line of direction)
2. The man steps backward with his right foot; the woman step forward with her left

Meas. 3:
Dance Ct.:
1. The man steps backward with his left foot; the woman steps forward with her right
2. The man steps backward with his right foot; the woman steps forward with her left

This position can be maintained as the couple travels around the room counter-clockwise as long as desired, then complete the last half of the turn as described below.

Couple Full Turn

Meas. 1: As above

Meas. 2: Counts 1, &, as in the Couple 1/2 Turn

Dance Ct.: 2   The man steps in place with his right foot; the woman steps in place with her left (the clockwise turn continues)

Meas. 3:

Dance Ct.: 1   The man steps to the left with his left foot; the woman steps in place with her right foot (the clockwise turn continues, now approximately a 3/4 turn)

2   The man steps in place with his right foot; the woman steps to the left with her left foot (the clockwise turn is completed)

Note: The Couple 1/2 and Full Turns can be done counter-clockwise by each person doing the other's footwork.

Arm Figures

Remember, all figures are broken down into segments which take the first three steps of one Basic Sequence (see measure 1 above) and are guided by the person in the man's position.

- **Outside Arch Under** — The man releases his right hand from the woman's shoulder while guiding her into a full turn to the right under uplifted arms (the woman's right, the man's left).

- **Inside Arch Under** — The man releases his right hand from the woman's shoulder, guiding her into a full turn to the left.

- **Walk Around** (Two-sequence figure)

    Step Sequence 1 — During one of the Arch Under figures above, the man moves forward and guides the woman to the right to right shoulder position, placing her right hand on his left waist.

    Step Sequence 2 — The man holds the woman's right hand at his waist with his right hand (releasing his left) as he continues forward and she circles clockwise behind him to arrive at his left side, facing the line of direction, and places her left hand in his which he has extended in front of her.

- **Exit from Walk Around** — Release the hand at the man's waist as the woman turns 1/2 to the left (or 1-1/2 to the right) under uplifted arms while the man guides her into basic position and changes the arm hold.

    Or on the last step of sequence 2 of the Walk Around, the man leans forward to guide the woman's right hand (held behind the man) to go up and over his head. At the beginning of the next sequence, the woman turns 1-1/2 to the right under both arms into basic position.

- **Woman Wrap to Man's Left Side** — The woman turns 1/2 right, in place while wrapping her right arm (his left) around her waist while her left (his right) passes over her head. Meanwhile, the man guides her to his left side. A 1-1/2 turn into Wrap is possible by executing an Arch Under and catching the woman's free hand, guiding her quickly into Wrap.

Do the opposite arm work to Wrap at the man's right side.

- **Exit from Woman Wrap** — Release the outside hands as the woman turns 1/2 left under the uplifted inside arms into basic position.

  Release the inside hands as the woman turns 1/2 right, under uplifted outside arms.

  Do the opposite arm work to exit from a Woman's Wrap to the man's right.

- **Lock and Turn**

  Step Sequence 1 — The woman is guided into Outside Arch Under (1/2 or 1-1/2 turn) as the man moves his hand from her right shoulder to place her right hand at waist level. He moves to her side as she turns to end in a right-to-right shoulder position with the woman's left arm wrapped behind her. The man now faces the line of dance; the woman faces to the right of the line of dance.

  Step Sequence 2 — The couple circles each other 1/2 clockwise without advancing in the line of direction.

  Step Sequence 3 — The man circles clockwise behind the woman as he guides her into a full left turn in place under his uplifted left hand (holding her right) into a Wrap to his left.

Exit — The exit is the same as the exit from the Woman Wrap to the Man's Left.

- **Laces**

  Step Sequence 1 — The woman is guided into a single or double-turn Inside Arch Under as the man moves toward the center of the room and turns 1/2 right to end in open reverse position (i.e. both partners face to the right of the line of dance), holding hands at arms length.

  Step Sequence 2 — The man turns 1/2 left and moves to the outside under held hands as the woman circles 1/2 right, behind the man, to end in open position facing the line of direction.

  Step Sequence 3 — Repeat the Inside Arch Under as above, but from open position.

  Step Sequence 4 — Repeat sequence 2. The man keeps his held hand (man's left; woman's right) at waist level and Wraps to the woman's right.

  Exit 1 — Drop the hand hold at the waist and turn the woman as in the Exit from Woman Wrap to the Man's Right.

  Exit 2 — The man leans forward and escapes as in the Walk Around Exit.

COWBOY WALTZ

The Texas Waltz and Two-Step are done in a modified ballroom (closed) position (the man facing the line of direction). The man holds the woman's right hand with his left, extended to his left and slightly forward. His right hand is on top of her left shoulder and serves as the main guide for the dance. Her left hand is either drooped over his right elbow (her elbow hanging down), or, when familiar, her left thumb is hooked into his right belt loop.

Meas. 1:
Dance Ct.: 1 The man steps forward with his left foot; the woman steps backward with her right
2 Same with opposite feet
3 Repeat count 1
Meas. 2: Repeat measure 1 on the opposite feet

This can be repeated as the couple travels around the room counter-clockwise as long as desired.

Outside Arch Under

Meas. 1: The woman makes a full turn to her own right, going under uplifted arms (the man's right; the woman's left). This should take all three steps in the measure.

Inside Arch Under

The Inside Arch Under is not usually done immediately following an Outside Arch, but on any measure 2.

Meas. 2: The woman makes a full turn to her left, going under uplifted arms (the man's right; the woman's left).